27 Apples

poems by

Chloe Viner

Finishing Line Press
Georgetown, Kentucky

27 Apples

Copyright © 2016 by Chloe Viner
ISBN 978-1-63534-021-1 First Edition
All rights reserved under International and Pan-American Copyright Conventions.
No part of this book may be reproduced in any manner whatsoever without written permission from the publisher, except in the case of brief quotations embodied in critical articles and reviews.

ACKNOWLEDGMENTS

Some of the poems in '27 Apples' have been previously published.
"What Will You Have", "Apple Picking", and "Mortar and Men" by Grey Wolf Publishing in their collection, *Legends*.
"Waiting" by *Grey Sparrow Journal*
"She is a Library" by *Down and the Dirt*
"For a Spell'" in Randolph Vermont's *Poemtown Collection*.

Publisher: Leah Maines

Editor: Christen Kincaid

Cover Art: Chloe Viner

Author Photo: Shane Collins

Cover Design: Elizabeth Maines

Printed in the USA on acid-free paper.
Order online: www.finishinglinepress.com
        also available on amazon.com

Author inquiries and mail orders:
Finishing Line Press
P. O. Box 1626
Georgetown, Kentucky 40324
U. S. A.

Table of Contents

Shrunk	1
Toothless	2
What Will You Have?	3
To Dye For	4
Hairdo	5
Waiting	6
Trying to Find You	7
Syrup and Semen	8
Winter	9
Reincarnation	10
For a Spell	11
Old Hat	12
Doors	13
Apple Picking	14
Clipped Wings	15
Last Night	16
Beast	17
She Is a Library	18
Mortar and Men	19
A Love Poem	20
I Don't Answer	21
Wax	23
Veteran	24
Abacus	25
Mourning	26
Black and White	27
Panic Attack	28

*Dedicated to Cheryl Hanna, Erica Lewis
and all those who have lost their battle with depression.*

Shrunk

I could have lived forever
in the charcoal smudges
of her curls
the blackness of her eyes
between iris and an expanse of white
on the tip of her nose
skating across the smooth surface
of her fingernails
sleeping in the curled crevice of her
left ear

I could have spent a lifetime
living in her sheets
bathing in her sweat
climbing the expanse of her thighs
taking bubble baths in her belly button

But I grew and thus no longer fit
when she realized this,
she left.

I had become so small it took
seventeen years for anyone to see me
as I climbed out of curls, belly buttons, ears
and grew back to
my original size.

Toothless

I awoke to find my teeth eaten away
parasites feasting in my molars
no words I spoke could undo damage
no dentist could repair or replace
what was taken away in the night
like when I was raped:
words eaten away
questions I didn't want to answer
so I stayed silent, toothless, wordless
awoke to see parts of me gone
as though someone poured acid
on my body in the night
the holes weeping
tears my face couldn't produce
until one day someone new looked at me
and he didn't see the holes,
he saw the *whole*.

What Will You Have?

"A vodka martini with a twist,"
she says, likes she's ordering
a night of passion in the bedroom
and cuff links
by the bathroom sink
but really she just ordered
a headache, a loose bra, and mascara marks
strewn across her face like scars from a battle.

The bartender collects their loneliness, tips in a jar
squirrels them away for future use
like that divorcee he served six rounds and
the shadow of tomorrow,
goes home and wonders
"am I a salesman, a doctor, or a priest?"
in the end the man who pours the drinks
is all three
or, when the glass empties,
he is none.

To Dye For

They came out of the dye transformed
little white orbs
she wished she could
become a chameleon
alas, she was no Easter egg
dreams washed down the drain
with red hair dye
a jar of sea glass on the windowsill
all that remains
of her youth.

Traces her lips with red pencil
screams into a full sink
emerges, edges blurred
not a beautiful white orb changing color
disarray dripping dye down her white gown,
losing hope in any last chances for
transformation.

Hairdo

She puts each thought in a curl of hair
Twists them into shape
observations, anecdotes, moments
power point from last Wednesday
the feeling of heels on pavement,
swept across her brow
last week's blind date conversation
tucked behind her left ear
watching the sunset from her bed
falls loose and tickles her neck
in her bun
three thousand five hundred thirty three moments.

As she ages, they fall out
walks, train rides, hotel brunches
remaining hairs cling to her scalp
refusing to let loose
insisting that the taste of chocolate
sound of rain
her wedding morning
be there when she dies.

Waiting

You talked to me the way rain talked to a
fifty-year old wooden banister
soaking into seams, filling holes
drops pooling over the edges of the beam

In the summer of your silence
dry wood cracked into splinters
like an elderly man's knuckles,
slivers of that silence
aged like a wine or a cheese
but no delicacy or subtle variations in that passage of time
everything muted
quiet crumbles in my mouth like stale pastry
sugar crystallized into snow flakes
slide down
like rain drops on the banister, siphoned off
all that's left, a pale shell of wood

I am left pacing in the dry dirt,
waiting for the rain
or am I waiting to hear you talk to me again?

Trying to Find You

It has been 27 apples
3 traffic tickets
and an election
since I last saw you.

Squirrels forage for the apple seeds
crumpled ballots degrade until ink seeps into soil
small saplings born of discarded votes
a speeding ticket becomes a mouse nest,
the rest of the world makes new beginnings

Flesh and wood and bone
tears and boxes and flowers
and us.

A widow places red irises at a grave
as I lie on the frozen ground and sink into the earth
trying to find you.

Syrup and Semen

She hands him the key, rusty but functional
like the others, he uses it to open her legs
sticky semen on her thighs
she wonders if anyone will find the
pin-sized keyhole in her back
unzip her spine,
latch onto the vertebrae and let loose in her blood stream

She eats until it aches
all this syrup and semen
still hollow,
a tree trunk eaten from the inside
branches reach outward
inside; ants, termites, lions eat
everything

Winter

Branches break under weight of wet snow
same as you, under every word I say
until the splinters of our bodies cover the forest floor
snapping under a doe's hoof as her fawn searches
for small patches of green
the same way you look at me
hoping something will sprout through ice
finding only a never-ending expanse of white

Put your auger down on the frozen pond
you will find no fish here,
looking at you from under the ice
mouths frozen in time
bubbles suspended like words of a
comic book hero
we will never break free of the page, of the ice,
of the words you keep waiting
to hear escape from my lips.

Reincarnation

She chose these things
sitting in the space between death and life
on a floating pink-laced sofa cushion
the whole world, a snow globe in her hand
chose the parents who would conceive her
chose each disappointment the way a cook
reaches for herbs, knowing what is needed
by tasting the batter, the soup, the dough
a dash of depression
dollop of anxiety
pinch of compassion
a whole cup of tenacity
she measured, leveled, whipped and mixed
until she could be poured into a dish, baked
come out of the oven, the belly, the sofa cushion
taste the dough of her life on her lips
and know what she would need
next time.

For a Spell

words climb out of the binding
letters tangle in bed sheets
sweat and vowels drip down my chest
sweet U lost under my left breast
angry Y stuck under the skin of my right palm
later when I face him
with I's grasped between my fingers,
Chinese fighting stars
I launch
until the tears that stream down the holes in his
face let loose the letters I need to
spell
goodbye.

Old Hat

Depression is boring
same patched gray top hat
as though I'm not used to it hanging by the door
dripping rain onto the wool carpet by now
carefully, I pack it for goodwill
drive as far as my car will take me for $12.80
leave it on the back deck behind the store
with oversized trash bags
but it's always waiting for me when I get home
my duty like a queen wears a crown
some days it is a small beret
others I drive home and there is nothing
but a giant hat
looming over the mountains
and I live here between the lint and gray fabric
muted by felt
buried by the rim
maybe tomorrow
maybe
tomorrow.

Doors

She did not know where the door led
only that it had not yet been opened
she felt the need to wait as if sleeping

Thinking that she might find the answer between the Z's of her snores
that if she opened it, everything inside her might tumble forward
lines of poetry, half-eaten meals, her first broken heart, canned laughter,
memories of Saturday afternoon walks
curls of hair from that time she got a pixie cut
tumbling into a heap at her feet
she turns the knob
but all that comes out is the smell of her grandparent's basement
beige carpet, small window overlooking the back parking lot
she doesn't find the tennis shoes she wore
to her first track meet in the fifth grade

She wishes someone would pick her up like a salt shaker
sprinkle all that residue out
so she could sort through it at her leisure
find the moments worth keeping
file them away between tax returns and late bills
always able to return to the green tab and
see sunburns, stomach aches, and her first kiss
the way she held old receipts
contemplating the purchase.

Apple Picking

Apple picking
while chickens dance
as though walking on hot coals
pecking beaks opening to squawk warnings as
feathers fall like raindrops,
we pick three ripe red Macintoshes.

Before apples had brand names
and chickens had cages,
there was a time of year when you could grow
'most anything'
eating ripe peaches on the door stoop
watching trees bend in the wind
and children run for cover
sneakers muddy,
a shy salamander
poking his head out of a pocket.

Now plants withered
earth black underfoot
cracked in every direction.

Behind the old shed
bird corpses and apple cores
but not a ripe peach in sight.

Clipped Wings

If you love the broken long enough
you end up collecting the fragments of yourself
like autumn leaves scattered across the road
losing pieces as cars and people trample through
unaware that that is your last memory stuck on the sole of their shoe
or the tire of their car
spinning away with the residue of you.

If you love the broken long enough
it is dancing on broken glass
leaving bloody footprints away from this place,
looking at you and seeing that you are
nothing
that you are supposed to be
mocking bird with clipped wings
that will never
sing.

Last Night

At my childhood home,
the fridge full of rotted food
sink overflowing with battered dishes
I got to work scrubbing surfaces, nothing came clean
harder I worked more the dishes piled,
rotted food spilled from the fridge onto the glistening floor
I could not save my childhood home
my ex-lover watched sadly
speaking too loudly, trying to be convivial

My father walked through the door
people and rotted fruit out of place
he accused me then,
I told him of twenty seven years' worth
of raw bleeding knuckles scrubbing dishes that never came clean,
he cried for me on the marble countertops but
never apologized.

I woke from this dream
to my husband, my home, a house void of parents
went to the kitchen
washed dishes until they sparkled in the light
the moon cast through our kitchen window over
three apple trees.

Beast

Depression won't be reasoned with
stubborn fifteen-year-old in class
unwilling to listen to the teacher
brakes on ice
that can't react to the press of your foot
jumping away in protest
causing you to skid into the snowbank
book already written, impervious to edits
dog who won't heal
no matter the leash or collar

A beast you cage each morning
padlock on metal beam
frothing at the mouth
she greets you at the door
regardless of lock or key
some days your husband returns home to find
bloody prints leading to half of you
the rest, nowhere to be found
others, you manage to tame it
make it silent for days or weeks,
dream of a day when you take the antique
rifle off its spot on the wall
aim the gun between the beast's eyes
and fire
but you have yet to find a way to
extract the beast
from your chest, and you are not going
anywhere
so for now
the beast stays.

She Is a Library

She bends the binding of her paperback thought
and eases herself in the margins
she tucks herself in between the sentences
and finds comfort in the periods and colons.

Mortar and Men

Materials don't matter
brick, mortar, hay, plaster, particle board
lost in the sound of construction
each hammered nail a symphony
each sweaty shout a dazzling lyric
so much can be found in the mundane
in the end, everything is made by
Mortar and Men
muscles flexing, the sun rises and sets in their arms

the rain and snow fall from their brows
every piece of the earth is
exuded from their skin.

A Love Poem

Your kiss is
that last sip of coffee:
sugar congealed
thickly sweet
the bitterness gone
as quickly as a robin taking flight from her nest
returning to feed her babes
as though she never took flight
that is the way you comfort me,
always perched curiously close to my open mouth
dropping in morsels of kindness and art
until my stomach is round
and there is no sense in leaving this twig bed of ours.

That winter the ice grew thick in patches
like an old man's hair
sprouting in unlikely places
underneath the ground we burrowed
making our home between tree roots and laughter
and you picked the acorns out of my hair
as I ran my fingers across the scar on your forearm
and we both remembered what it was like
before there were nests and burrows

we dissolve into the dirt
and the blooming tree turns us into leaves
but we never leave each other.

I Don't Answer

My grandmother was thirty, long black curls
hung herself on a visit home
my mother found her,
blood stains on the step stool
after, she jumped on the counter
when she needed cereal.

A Greek goddess
with her like
witnessing an inexplicable surgery
blood everywhere,
but a belief that organs would end up back
in the right spot

One Sunday afternoon,
tried to drown my mother in the
porcelain tub
pink rose petals on the walls
corpse of the cat limp on the floor
so my mother would know
what to expect.

Years later
my mentor
her nine-year-old son and eleven-year-old daughter
dark hair brushing shoulders,
brilliant, charismatic, voice on NPR-mother
ended her life
on the cold cement basement floor,
while they were at a Greek festival
eating baklava, dancing on grass
told them she was going to yoga,
mat and water bottle still on the
wooden chair by the door, waiting.

I was eighteen, motherless
asked "I'm still here?"
In a narrow hospital bed
vomiting black chunks of charcoal
held 72 hours
as if minutes and days might nourish me
fluorescent lights, packaged Jello, and distracted doctors
might fill me.

Ten years later
Sometimes, I still hear seductive tones,
siren on the rocks
urging me to crash into stony shore for reprieve.

I don't answer
readjust my sails
take in slack,
wrap my blisters in bandages,

the blood stains everything I touch
but I'm still here, touching it.

Wax

She liked riding on his shoulders
could reach the lower leaves of Oaks
before they turned red

She would take leaves home,
iron them between wax paper
forever sealed in that moment
She wondered if that could happen to her
frozen on her father's shoulders
mounted on a wall
or placed on a coffee table

not raked or piled,
hauled to the curb in over-sized trash bags.

Veteran

He came back on a Wednesday
pieces left along the way
in the dunes, trampled by combat boots
at an Afghani diner on the old red leather seats
sprinkled on his army cot,
washed off with layers of dirt
down the portable shower drain

Said "go ahead, scout, I'll catch you later"
drank coffee, black and sticky
thumbed cracked knuckles on plastic folding table
pictured his wife's blonde hair brushing his cheek
as she tossed in bed.

They brought his friend back in pieces
chunks of his left arm
discarded in dunes
wasn't just his friend,
was 23 percent of himself
mangled and buried with shots fired

He wished he had died
77 percent was doable
but he belonged in the sand, on tires
of re-commissioned Humvees
spinning away with
his mistakes.

Abacus

He grew up between
cement walls and metal gates
sleeping on an uneven mattress
twelve years old and cracking at the seams
just like him
washed his face in a silver bowl
urinated in front of fifty men
his mother the guard who didn't beat anyone
his father the overweight cellmate who left him alone
his sister the books he had to distract himself
a paper abacus he made to substitute for the calculator
they forbade him
hiding under the scratchy polyester blanket
counting to get to the right answer
days, meals, books, thoughts
always counting.

Mourning

Silver monogramed cufflinks
flimsy, pale, blue, wrinkled
the same as your face furrows
sun setting in the ocean
everything through the button hole
of time and space

I taste the absence in
whispers and shouts
basements and attics
sweep cobwebs aside
leave one large black spider
upside down
dead legs facing the ceiling.

Black and White

I am coal in the fire of this country's engine
construction workers wipe my residue from brows
shoes caked in my arms, teeth, strands of my hair
my blood, dust filling lungs of children
five hundred times, head down, same block
headphones, small jewel of ancestors who
lifted slabs of this country like Atlas
covered in fire ants and icicles
red and white of those beasts
the stripes on that flag
pinpricks of blue the stars we followed to get here
flip the collar
the hood of the sweatshirt,
the color of your skin
my blood paints the street
I am red instead of black
will you realize then I am the color of the flag
put down your butcher knife
and stop carving me?

Panic Attack

The air is thin
a mountain peak
no calming views
top of a 10,000 foot tower
liable to misplace a foot and plummet
limbs askew
broken remains
a tongue and fingernail
several feet away
noose around my throat
a dog on a collar with no choice
you cannot reason with someone on the battlefield
gun raised, focused on survival
every time I pull the trigger the bullet ricochets
and I wake in a pool of my own
blood and sweat
two Zanex and a rum and coke
dull the bullet-wound in my side
noose around my throat
but I can still feel the gallows
behind my back
as people cheer.

Chloe Viner's first chapbook, *Naked Under an Umbrella*, was published by Finishing Line Press in 2011. Her second chapbook, *What the Rain Said Last Night* was published by Future Cycle Press. This is her third chapbook.

www.ingramcontent.com/pod-product-compliance
Lightning Source LLC
LaVergne TN
LVHW041510070426
835507LV00012B/1465